CLASSICAL THEMES FOR TWO

Arrangements by Peter Deneff

ISBN 978-1-5400-1411-5

7777 W. BLUEMOUND RD. P.O. BOX 13819 MILWAUKEE, WI 53213

In Australia Contact:
Hal Leonard Australia Pty. Ltd.
4 Lentara Court
Cheltenham, Victoria, 3192 Australia
Email: ausadmin@halleonard.com.au

ACADEMIC FESTIVAL OVERTURE

FLUTES

By JOHANNES BRAHMS

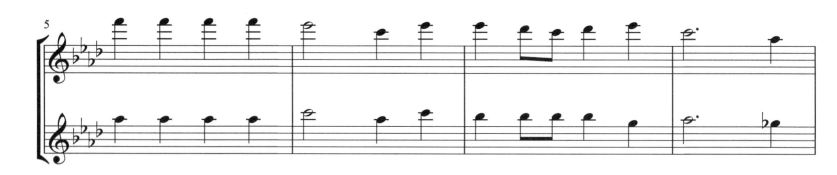

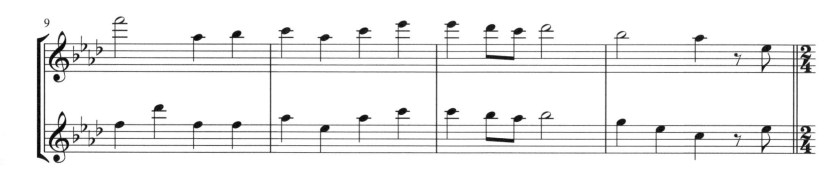

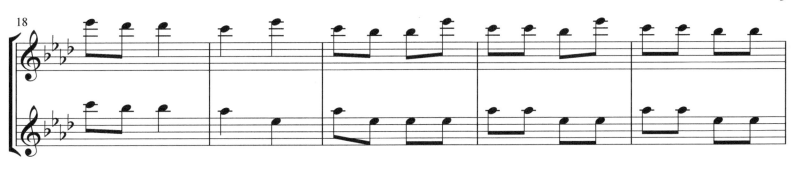

AIR
from WATER MUSIC

FLUTES

By GEORGE FRIDERIC HANDEL

Andante con moto

(small notes optional)

To Coda

AIR ON THE G STRING
from ORCHESTRAL SUITE NO. 3 IN D MAJOR, BWV 1068

FLUTES

By JOHANN SEBASTIAN BACH

BLUE DANUBE WALTZ

FLUTES

By JOHANN STRAUSS, JR.

Moderately

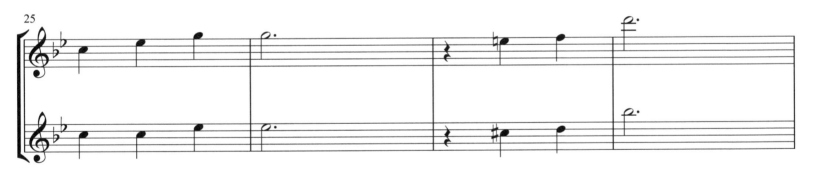

CANON IN D

FLUTES

By JOHANN PACHELBEL

CLAIR DE LUNE
from SUITE BERGAMASQUE

By CLAUDE DEBUSSY

FLUTES

EINE KLEINE NACHTMUSIK
(Second Movement Theme: "Romance")

FLUTES

By WOLFGANG AMADEUS MOZART

FLOWER DUET

from LAKMÉ

FLUTES

By LÉO DELIBES

HALLELUJAH CHORUS
from MESSIAH

FLUTES

By GEORGE FRIDERIC HANDEL

Allegro

(small note optional)

rit.

rit.

HORNPIPE
from WATER MUSIC

FLUTES

By GEORGE FRIDERIC HANDEL

Allegro maestoso

HUNGARIAN DANCE NO. 5

By JOHANNES BRAHMS

FLUTES

JESU, JOY OF MAN'S DESIRING
from CANTATA 147

FLUTES

By JOHANN SEBASTIAN BACH

MARCH
from THE NUTCRACKER

FLUTES

By PYOTR IL'YICH TCHAIKOVSKY

March tempo

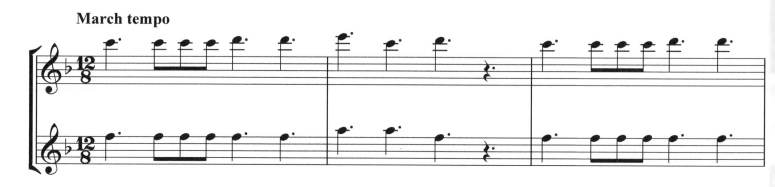

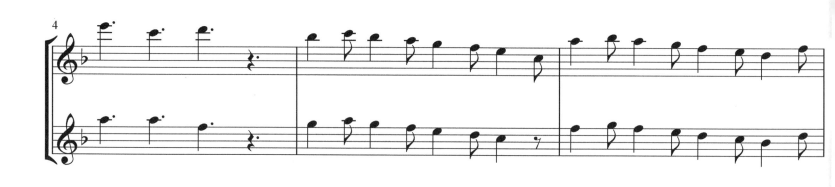

MINUET IN G
from ANNA MAGDALENA NOTEBOOK

FLUTES

By CHRISTIAN PETZOLD
formerly attributed to J.S. Bach

ODE TO JOY
from SYMPHONY NO. 9 IN D MINOR

FLUTES

By LUDWIG VAN BEETHOVEN

MORNING
from PEER GYNT

FLUTES

By EDVARD GRIEG

Allegretto pastorale

PICTURES AT AN EXHIBITION
(Promenade)

FLUTES

By MODEST MUSSORGSKY

POMP AND CIRCUMSTANCE
March No. 1

FLUTES

By EDWARD ELGAR

RONDEAU
from SUITE DE SYMPHONIE

By JEAN-JOSEPH MOURET

FLUTES

SHEEP MAY SAFELY GRAZE

from CANTATA 208

FLUTES

By JOHANN SEBASTIAN BACH

THE SURPRISE SYMPHONY
(Symphony No. 94, Second Movement Theme)

FLUTES

By FRANZ JOSEPH HAYDN

Andante

SYMPHONY NO. 7
(Second Movement Theme)

FLUTES

By LUDWIG VAN BEETHOVEN

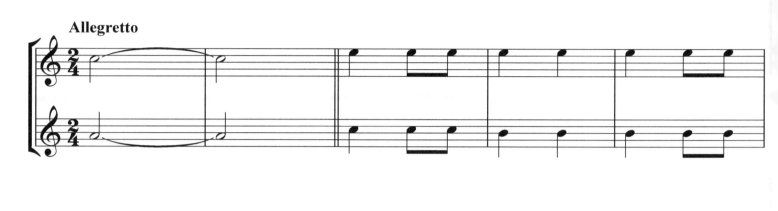

TRUMPET VOLUNTARY
(Prince of Denmark's March)

FLUTES

By JEREMIAH CLARKE

WILLIAM TELL OVERTURE
(Theme)

FLUTES

By GIOACHINO ROSSINI

Allegro vivace